PUNDAMENTALIST

1,000 jokes you probably haven't heard before

GARY DELANEY

HEADLINE

First published in 2020
by HEADLINE PUBLISHING GROUP

3

Cataloguing in Publication Data is available from the British Library

Hardback ISBN 978 1 4722 7743 5

Designed and typeset by EM&EN
Printed and bound in Great Britain by Clays Ltd, Elcograf S.p.A.

Headline's policy is to use papers that are natural, renewable and recyclable
products and made from wood grown in well-managed forests and other
controlled sources. The logging and manufacturing processes are expected
to conform to the environmental regulations of the country of origin.

HEADLINE PUBLISHING GROUP
An Hachette UK Company
Carmelite House
50 Victoria Embankment
London EC4Y 0DZ

www.headline.co.uk
www.hachette.co.uk

Foreword

Quartet.

I'd like to start this book with a joke about crowbars, as they always make a great opener.

'I'm never jogging behind a council van in winter again,' he said through gritted teeth.

A friend of mine was killed in an accident at a florist's, so now every year we tie a car to the lamppost outside.

My girlfriend's arse is like a peach: hairy and makes a horrible yogurt.

50% of people who go to watch The Cure actually end up watching Placebo, and enjoy it just as much.

Oh no! Just sent a picture of my knob to everyone in my address book. Not only embarrassing but also cost a fortune in stamps.

I didn't want to buy a hammock, but the salesman was very persuasive, and I'm easily swayed.

I coughed on the tube, and a suicide bomber got up and moved to the next carriage.

I nearly lost my job as a roofer when I was caught masturbating on my first day, luckily my boss said I could wipe the slate clean.

Pundamentalist

Set Password: Tiny_Tim.

Sorry, password contains an invalid character.

If you write 'rotaluclac' on your boobs and then turn upside down it says 'calculator'.

My golf instructor said I need to work on my follow through. I said, 'Is it my golf swing?' He said, 'No, you've got shit down the back of your trousers.'

Last night I had beef stew with dumplings.

I shouldn't call her that, but she's a big girl.

I owe so much money to my herb seller that he's threatened to send round the bay leafs.

We can't even afford a garden, so when my
girlfriend bought us a trampoline I hit the roof.

Gentlemen, if you think your partner's vagina
is rather large it's important that you never let on
to that fact and believe me I know as I once
put my foot in it.

My French pen friend just said 'Le monde',
which means the world to me.

It's ironic that to claim disability benefit you
have to jump through a lot of hoops.

Pundamentalist

Does anyone know if it's safe to dye your pubes?
It's a bit of a grey area.

I went to see an acupuncturist.
When I got home, my voodoo doll was dead.

Actors have got Equity, magicians have got the
Magic Circle, but it's a shame ventriloquists don't
have anyone to speak for them.

I used to be into ham radio, but all I could hear
was crackling.

The study of why triangular sandwiches taste
better is known as trigonomnomnometry.

I was at an Italian zoo with a Christian friend of mine, so I thought 'When in Rome . . .' and pushed him into the lions.

Oedipus, what a motherfucker.

People say I'm unnecessarily vindictive, so they go on the list.

I used to run the Iranian Madam Tussauds, but it was impossible to make a prophet.

My grandad was killed by a Zulu. He was having a shit at Whipsnade and the roof collapsed.

Pundamentalist

I've a Welsh friend who says when he can't sleep
he counts sheep, then gets horny, has a wank,
and nods right off.

I was actually Birmingham Memory Man of the
year, back in 1980 something.

Don't die a virgin, otherwise when you go to
heaven you have to marry a suicide bomber.

I shoved a glass eyeball up my arse, which wasn't
a good idea, with the benefit of hindsight.

It was tough growing up in the '70s. Mum was alone,
Dad was in and out of nick. Nick was furious.

When Grandad found out he'd got palsy his
face fell.

I don't like sex in the shower. It's slippy, dangerous
and one of the worst things about prison.

A clock from a Salvador Dali painting goes into a
bar. The barman says, 'Why the long face?'

When I open the fridge and the light comes on
I like to pretend a sausage has just had a really
good idea. 'Why not have me with mash?'

When are hairdressers going to release the results
of that big survey they've been doing on where
people are going on holiday?

Pundamentalist

I recently met up with loads of other supportive heavy drinkers, dipsomaniacs, winos, drunkards and lushes at my Alcoholics Synonymous meeting.

I spent the afternoon in the park mentally undressing women. I find they are less likely to complain, if you do pretend to be mental.

Did you know that if the entire population of China was to walk past your house in single file, that would be really creepy.

I visited a Mosque recently and I was disappointed to find the reason you have to take your shoes off isn't because there's a bouncy castle inside.

Gary Delaney

I asked someone to send me an audio file, and then
a bloke turned up at my house explaining why
vinyl was loads better than digital.

I went to see a Polish Pink Floyd tribute band.
Not only were they cheaper but they played
The Wall in half the time.

I went to the zoo to watch the monkeys wanking,
then I went to watch the crocodiles and I was
still wanking.

I remember sitting in psychology class learning
about Pavlov, thinking those stupid dogs, and then
the bell went and we all had lunch.

Pundamentalist

Red sky at night: light of shorter wavelengths
is being dissipated by water vapour and
atmospheric dust.
Red sky in the morning: same.

I'm sitting at home, and this guy knocks on my
door. 'Have you ever considered an alternative
energy supplier?' I'm like, 'No, I'm quite happy
with food.'

I've got the memory of an elephant. I remember
one time I went to the zoo and saw an elephant.

I recently launched a book aimed at 9–12 year olds,
and I'm proud to say I hit one of the little shits.

I recently tried anal bleaching. It was tricky to do, but eventually I managed to bleach every object in the house in alphabetical order.

Uri Geller, surprisingly hard to stab.

I'd have five pounds on the Dalai Lama, if I was a Tibetan man.

I went on a positive thinking course. It was shit.

I went to see the stalactites at Cheddar Gorge and our guide asked us not to try and crack one off and she wasn't even that attractive.

But I still managed.

It was very dark.

Pundamentalist

This morning I went to a meeting of my premature
ejaculators support group.
Turns out it's tomorrow.

The Paralympics taught us that sometimes
we should stop and put ourselves in the place
of people with disabilities. And I have to say,
those parking spaces are brilliant.

I bought a book to look up minor operations,
but it wasn't much use as the appendix had
been removed.

I've been trying to recapture my lost youth.
I really must get that cellar door fixed.

As a child I was made to walk the plank.
We couldn't afford a dog.

Gary Delaney

Bought a chameleon, lost it.

I had a chocolate bar and inside the wrapper
it said, 'You're a loser'. I wouldn't have minded
had there been some sort of competition on.
To make things worse it was a Boost.

I've been trying to persuade my girlfriend to
sexually stimulate me with her keyring but she
just keeps fobbing me off.

When my girlfriend suggested we try playing
doctors and nurses I was really hoping for
something sexier than being left in a corridor for
two days.

Pundamentalist

I went to a swingers' club. The doorman goes,
'It's £15 to get in or you can pay £20, that includes
a meal.' I paid £20, went in, and an oiled naked man
comes up to me and says, 'Hello, my name's Emile.'

A friend of mine was going on and on about how
good his orthopaedic shoe is, but I think he's built
it up too much.

When I heard you could now be a sperm donor
by post, I came in a jiffy.

A friend of mine said, 'If I text another man and
put a kiss at the end is that a bit gay?'
I said, 'What are you texting him?'
He said, 'A picture of my cock.'

In Norfolk the marriage guidance service is called Related.

In Cornwall jokes about inbreeding get 20% more applause.

I accidentally filled the escort with diesel. She died.

I don't like people who complain about breast feeding in public.
'I don't want to see it.'
Or 'that's disgusting.'
Or 'you can't do that you're not a woman',
'and that's not a baby'
'and that's definitely not milk.'

Pundamentalist

The Archbishop of Canterbury recently said
he couldn't support gay marriage without first
having a mandate. Honestly, if he's that bothered
I'll go out with him.

I always worry when a woman sees me naked
for the first time that she's just going to scream
and run out of the park.

Traffic news: A lorry carrying a giant Scrabble set
has overturned on the M25, motorists are warned
there could be large Qs.

I've warned people about the dangers of auto-erotic
asphyxiation until I'm blue in the face.

Gary Delaney

My girlfriend said she wanted to try some new condoms with something special inside to boost her pleasure. I said, 'Ooh what's that?' and she said, 'Other men's cocks.'

I asked the vet, 'What can I do, I think my dog's racist – he keeps barking at the Asian man next door?' The vet said, 'Muzzle him?' I said, 'I don't know but he's got a beard.'

I was disappointed to find that *Dunkirk* isn't a biography of William Shatner.

The Make-A-Wish foundation should really be called the 'No, Make Another Wish Foundation'.

I was in the garden with my girlfriend earlier and saw the 18-year-old girl next door all dolled up ready to go out clubbing. My girlfriend said, 'Do you know what? At that age I can really see myself in her.' Which is weird because I was thinking the exact same thing.

My Uncle Derek was found dead with a belt round his neck and a dildo up his arse. At his funeral, the vicar said we'll always remember him for his charity work. Wrong.

I once had a one night stand and I didn't get an erection. That isn't cool. Luckily the woman I was with was really understanding, and she just said, 'Don't worry, that used to happen to me.'

Gary Delaney

I was in town earlier and saw people collecting for Parkinson's, and they were shaking tins which I thought was a bit insensitive.

Because people collect money for anything nowadays and call it a charity, the other day I saw a woman collecting for reconstructive vaginal surgery following the birth of her eight children. There she was, outside Tesco, waving her bucket.

You know what it's like when you're wanking off 3 bus drivers at once, and it's taking ages, and then suddenly . . .

I was watching a really weird porn film the other day, that was just a fat man crying and wanking at the same time, and then I realised that I hadn't turned the telly on.

Pundamentalist

I think my favourite grime artist is probably the one who writes 'Clean me' on dirty white vans.

I saw a list of 100 books to read before you die, and I've only read 5 of them, so I've got a good few years left.

David Beckham could always slot a corner expertly into place, but couldn't manage the rest of the jigsaw.

The inventor of the progress bar managed to do 99% of it really quickly, but the last bit took him ages.

In Scotland it will soon be illegal to give a smack to children, but not to sell it to them.

Wearing an armband is considered a good way
to show your respects for someone who's died,
unless they drowned, in which case it's insensitive.

I once applied for a job as a mustard cutter but
unfortunately I wasn't quite good enough.

Britain's oldest dental hygienist has died aged 93.
The British Dental Association have removed a
plaque in her honour.

When I accidentally broke one of the exhibits
at the grenade museum, you could have heard
a pin drop.

Pah! The publisher has just rejected my
autobiography. That's the story of my life.

Don't sniff Creosote. It's a gateway drug.

Urologists, always thinking about number one.

One of my friends stole my platform shoes, and I know who it is, because now he can't look me in the eye.

I watched a documentary about black holes on the Discovery channel. I didn't want to, but I got sucked in.

If someone invented a cure for OCD they could clean up.

Just watching 2001. Honestly, it's PC gone mad.

Gary Delaney

I've just stolen all your laxatives. I shit you not.

I've just found out the surgeon carried out a lobotomy against my wishes, and now I've got half a mind to complain.

I sponsored a child in Africa. It's been five years now, and he's still sober.

I think this Rorschach bloke must have been some sort of closet homosexual. Every single inkblot seems to be just big burly men having sex!

To be honest when I was warned this film contained 'adult themes', I was hoping for more sex, and less about mortgages.

Pundamentalist

There are two typos of people in the world, those who notice spelling mistakes, and those who don't.

I remember one time at school we had a spelling bee. And also an ant who was good at sums.

Good News: I'm working from home today!
Bad News: I'm a fireman.

Just heard one of the athletes say that the London 2012 Paralympics made huge steps for the disabled, which can't have helped.

Apple Farmers who are too scared to diversify should just grow a pear.

Cockney A: I just bought some suncream from that pretty chemist.

Cockney B: Factor Two?

Cockney A: No, I just bought the suncream.

I've got the attention span of a gold . . . finger, he's the man, the man with the Midas touch.

I'm going to write a 'fuck it' list of things I can't be bothered to do before I die.

Reverend Spooner has asked me to remind everyone that the cocks go black tonight.

I had a nut roast the other day. I'm not vegan, I was just wearing leather trousers.

Pundamentalist

I'm now 20 hours into my sponsored semaphore marathon. Unfortunately I'm starting to flag quite badly.

Me: 'I now declare this bomb disposal school open.'
cuts red ribbon with giant scissors
Instructor: 'No, I said blue ribbon, BLUE!!'
KABOOM!!

A horse goes into a pub, the barman says, 'Why the long face?' The horse says, 'Because this is a Wetherspoons.'

I've written to the Royal Mail to complain about my post being stolen, and to make sure they see it, I've put it inside a birthday card.

My wife and I are a great match, for example
I've got a 9 inch penis, and she doesn't know
which way round to hold a ruler.

I shouldn't have got Patrick Swayze to redesign
the nursery. He's put the cot right in the middle
of the room.

I saw a man with a sandwich board saying,
'Repent you're sin's the end of the world is nigh',
and I thought, 'That's a bad sign.'

I can count the number of DIY accidents I've had
on the fingers of one hand.
Two.

Pundamentalist

A friend of mine's been suffering from paranoid
delusions and thinks he a Chocolate Orange.
I worry he's going to be sectioned.
Poor Terry.

My dad's been suffering from seizures.
So far they've take his car, his house and his boat.

Of course the best part of having an argument
is making up afterwards with hot angry sex,
but if anything that made the traffic warden
even more cross.

I was at the dentist's. He said, 'I have to warn you,
this is going to hurt.' I said, 'What is it?' He said,
'Your wife thinks I've got a bigger cock.' I said,
'You think that, but she doesn't know which way
round to hold a ruler.'

Gary Delaney

I used to go out with a traffic warden who was really into S&M. One time she put nipple clamps on me, and it cost £200 to get them removed.

I tried one of those Park 'n' Ride schemes the other day. Or as some people call it 'dogging'.

I'm a lot sportier than I might look, in fact I picked up a little niggle at the gym the other day.
I mean he pronounces it Nigel.

My wife always cheats when she's on a diet.
She hides little bars of chocolate all round the house and fucks other men.

Pundamentalist

I found out two new things this week.
One: sperm isn't actually good for your skin,
and two: my dermatologist has been struck off.
So that's the last time I go to his caravan.

A friend of mine said that if you look up the word
pedantic in the dictionary there's a picture of me
next to it, but there isn't.

I don't carry a donor card. I find it depressing
enough the amount of women who've rejected
my organ whilst I'm alive.

People who say that ketamine should be banned
should get down off their high horse.

One time the teacher asked me for a word with four Is, so I said, 'Mississippi', and he said, 'No, I mean I want to have a word, you speccy twat.'

One time I persuaded my little brother to swallow a torch. It was worth it just to see his little face light up.

I'm not saying my wife's embarrassed about me, but at our wedding I was only invited to the evening do.

My wife got herself a rampant rabbit. I wouldn't say it's her favourite sex toy, but it's definitely up there.

Pundamentalist

We've been trying to recapture the sex life we had when we were younger, so the other day I sent her a dick pic, and she texted back 'unsubscribe'.

When I suggested to my wife we try using a strap on she was right behind me.

I like to think of my wife as a trophy wife, because her ears stick out, and she's got the previous winners' names tattooed down her back.

I joined a fisting club. Not something I'm particularly into, I'm just trying to widen the circle of my friends.

When my wife's away my favourite thing to do is to poo with the door open, and really surprise the postman.

When I turned 40 I was overweight, out of shape and thought I wasn't the sort of person who could ever run a marathon. Now, just six years later, I also know that my observation skills are spot on.

I have this terrible recurring dream where I'm trying to divide 1 by 3.

Still waiting for the results of my leprosy test.
I don't know whether they're going to write to me, or just give me a bell.

Pundamentalist

I can't sleep at night unless the door is open
just a crack, but apparently 'that's not allowed
in this prison'.

People say the guy who sold me invisible hearing
aids is a con-man, but I won't hear a bad word said
about him.

I had a nightmare on the motorway getting here,
and luckily that woke me up.

I bought a vegan friend of mine a fancy cookbook
but he said he couldn't accept it because it was
leatherbound which meant it was too heavy for
him to lift.

A vegan friend of mine just offered me a cup of tea with a splash of his homemade nut milk and now I don't want tea anymore.

I'm not saying I was an ugly child, but I had to give paedophiles sweets.

My hairdresser's a dwarf, so I'm always worried about saying the wrong thing. Last time he said, 'Short back and sides?' and I said, 'Really? I hadn't noticed'.

I bought an alcoholic ginger beer. He wasn't pleased.

'The Disclaimers' would be a great tribute band. 'We are nothing to do with those ginger Scottish guys.'

I got one of those anti-bullying wristbands.

Didn't buy it, I nicked it off a ginger kid.

'I saw a stripper taking drugs earlier.'

'Smoking crack?'

'Yes, and her tits were pretty good as well.'

I've got a new job playing the triangle in a reggae band, and ting.

Never try and use a Ouija board to contact the ghost of a dyslexic.

'Q, P, V, L, R, F.'

'Is that you, Steve?'

Gary Delaney

The instructions on my microwave meal say stir and recover. How tiring do they think stirring actually is?

Why did the chicken use a Ouija board?
To get to the other side.

The Chair of the Dyslexic society was given an OBE, he said, 'What's the point? I can't play the bloody thing.'

I'm not saying I'm unlucky but when I went to DFS to buy a sofa, the sale had finished.

I'm still a bit shaken up. I was involved in quite a violent mugging the other day, but on the plus side I did make a few quid.

Pundamentalist

I wish the Germans had a word for the pleasure you get when someone tries to use the word 'Schadenfreude' and gets it wrong.

My cousin always introduces himself as Stephen with a PH, and that's because he's slightly acidic.

I slept with a schizophrenic girl, which as far as I'm concerned counts as a threesome.

One time I got a concussion from being punched in the temple. Mind you it was probably my fault for calling the Rabbi a cunt.

When they buried the man who invented Tetris, the whole cemetery disappeared.

Malcolm X chose that name rather than admit he'd accidentally put a kiss at the end of a text message.

I tell you what really boils my piss: hotel room kettles.

The lamb chops I've just bought are described as having been reared in Wales. I thought that was just a racist stereotype.

I once went to a camouflage swingers party. Everyone threw their khakis into a big bowl.

I used to really like paedophile jokes but now I think they're getting a bit old.

Pundamentalist

My dad loves playing Guess Who with the grandkids. He hasn't got the board game, he just can't remember what they're called.

'Doctor, Doctor, I'm addicted to fucking dogs.'

'Have you tried patches?'

'What's he, a poodle?'

I used to play around with time machines when I was older.

I was thrown out of my cloning exam for copying the kid next to me.

If anyone's got any tips on how to reverse cheap plastic surgery, I'm all ears.

I bet Dracula does all his shopping online, just so he can keep clicking on 'Your Account'.

My friend Jack Hughes went to France, but whenever he introduced himself to people they got all defensive.

I just got a parking ticket outside the Children's Television Workshop. Apparently it's Kermit holders only.

Kids today would be shocked to know that in the '80s you could find porn in bushes, and also the other way round.

I told my girlfriend I don't want to go to an '80s fancy dress party, but she remains adamant.

Pundamentalist

Brian Blessed has his own sign language
interpreter with really big hands.

Honestly, that roadrunner's pretty selfish. It's all
meep, meep, meep.

'A book about grammar? You shouldn't of.'

I've been going out with an English teacher
which is a bit awkward because she keeps
correcting my grammar during sex.
I'm like, 'Who's the daddy? Who's the daddy?'
And she's, 'No, the daddy's whom?'
I said, 'Suck it good, bitch.'
And she's, 'No, it's suck it well, bitch.'
And she gets particularly annoyed at my improper
use of the colon.

Tom Cruise could have made a lot more films if he wasn't constantly getting caricatures of his face done in Leicester Square.

I've just written 'You have no new messages' on a piece of paper, put it in a bottle and thrown it far out to sea.

I bought my kid some medicine for his ADHD. On the side of the bottle it said 'concentrate.' I thought, if he could do that . . .

Technically shoplifting from the Apple store only counts as scrumping.

People have tried to distract me with tiny mints, but I will not fall for diversionary tic tacs.

Pundamentalist

Emails are like testicular cancer: if you don't check your junk you might miss something important.

I've just been to the mobile library and borrowed a Nokia for three weeks.

I bought an advent calendar for Jehovah's Witnesses, behind every door somebody tells you to fuck off.

My uncle's a lion tamer. When he went bankrupt they took nearly everything, but at least he's still got his pride.

A friend of mine said I really must come round and eat his wife's beef wellington, and now I don't know if I've agreed to a dinner party or swinging.

Gary Delaney

The Jehovah's Witnesses used to constantly bang on my door at all hours and eventually it got so bad I had to soundproof the cellar.

Despite promising I wouldn't, I've gone abseiling without my instructor, and now I feel like I've let myself down.

My grandad died following a massive stroke. It was his own fault really, he should never have tried petting that lion.

I'm trying to learn to be a more sensitive lover. I got a DVD on how to improve your foreplay technique. It was really good. I had to fast forward through the boring bit at the beginning.

Pundamentalist

Coma is a very negative way of looking at things,
I prefer 'One more sleep 'til Christmas'.

Old lady names are very much back in fashion
at the minute, like Lily or Elsie or Rose, and we
wanted something like that for our daughter,
but we couldn't decide. So in the end we just
called her Nan.

I told her she'll grow into it.

My married friends would always tell me there's
someone out there for everyone, and I'd think,
wow, she must be a right slag.

'Knock Knock.'

'Who's there?'

'Grandad.'

'Shit, stop the funeral!'

Grandad asked me how to print on his new computer. I said, 'Just Ctrl P.' He said, 'I haven't been able to do that for years.'

There's a new celebrity magazine for the elderly, it's called 'Hello?', 'Hello?' . . . 'HELLO!'

I went to see Walt Disney on Ice. Bit disappointing, it's just an old bloke in a freezer.

Dave drowned so at his funeral we got him a wreath in the shape of a lifebelt.
Well it's what he would have wanted.

Pundamentalist

My girlfriend says I'm not very romantic.
The other day we were kissing on the sofa.
She said, 'How about we take this into the
bedroom?' I said, 'OK, you get the other end.'

My girlfriend and I are trying for a baby. Her mum's
agreed to help out, just until I get hard.

Sex education lessons at our school were pretty
weird. The teacher made us shout out rude words
to get it out of our system, like bum, willy, cocks.
And we had to carry on doing that until he came.

I bought a really nice 12 year old scotch.
Obviously his parents weren't pleased.

Gary Delaney

Nan always said that when she was young, she never had to worry about leaving her back door open. What a slag!

When I was a teenager my bedroom was so messy my mum used to say, 'You'll never get any self respecting girl to come back here', but luckily those weren't the ones I was going after.

I bought a slimming magazine in WH Smith's. I didn't read it, I just wanted a big bar of Galaxy for £1.

'I bought some fancy pens at a nudist art shop.'
'Felt tips?'
'No, but I touched a couple of bollocks.'

Pundamentalist

According to the vet, my cat's in heat. I didn't even know she was famous.

I live next door to a family of anorexic agoraphobics. I bet they've got a few skeletons in the closet.

I once met a girl who confused a tube of KY jelly with Superglue. I asked how it happened, but sadly her lips were sealed.

The other night I saw a couple weaving all over the street. I said, 'Honestly, get a loom!'

In Scotland the forbidden fruit is fruit.

When England played Poland at Wembley, there were thirty thousand Polish fans in the crowd and I thought, well fair play to them, if I'd built it, I'd want to have a look around as well.

I'm not saying people are oversensitive nowadays but this Winnie The Pooh book came with a Tigger warning.

Ironically a cure for premature ejaculation just can't come soon enough.

My thirteen-year-old cousin has already started taking heroin. It's amazing, isn't it? They shoot up so fast these days.

Pundamentalist

I spent most the afternoon hanging out at the swimming baths. And then somebody told me and I tucked it back in again.

I used to work at Waterstones. One day a guy came in asking if we had any audio books with subtitles. I thought, hang on, that's a book.

The circus near me held a competition to find the best contortionist. So I entered myself and won.

I hate people who phone me up just to complain about the weather, which is why I lost my job at mountain rescue.

I was at a station the other day that had a piano on the platform, so I had a little tinkle on it, which saved me 30p.

I think if I was to try revenge porn, I'd just post naked pictures of myself online so everybody would know how low my ex's standards really were.

The other day a woman described me as a bit of a looker. Well voyeur was the actual word that she used.

My last girlfriend was always trying to put me down, which is just one of the hazards of going out with a vet.

Pundamentalist

The area in a Nandos between the front and back door is called the peri peri-neum.

I like to judge my weight by my BMI. As long as I weigh less than a small plane, I think it's fine.

When writing a story about losing your virginity, it's important to always put it in the first person.

I pulled a sickie the other day. Just one of the perks of working at the hospital.

The other day my girlfriend and I had great make up sex. Well I say that, she was out and I stuck her lipstick up my arse.

Last night I had to get towed home because Ratty and Moley were too pissed.

My girlfriend's a cat person. She's got fishy breath, shits in a tray and disappears for days at a time.

Dolphins who die without any money are given a porpoise funeral.

So the other day I was chewing on some monkey nuts and now I'm banned from the zoo.

My sister gave birth on a trampoline, and I'm pleased to say she now has a bouncing baby boy.

Pundamentalist

I remember when the optician first told me I needed glasses. Well I say optician, it could have been anyone really.

I got myself a Corgi boiler, and that shut the yappy little fucker up for good.

Ghosts make 'woooooo' noises because they are naturally very scarcastic.

I thought I'd never really understand angles, but then I did a complete 360.

I recently had my first Five Guys, and then went for a burger.

Gary Delaney

I'm best known as a comedian, but not a lot of people know that I once sang in the West End, which completely ruined Macbeth.

I must be worst hangman ever. I've let everybody down.

The inventor of Ribena intended for it be drunk undiluted, but his proposals were watered down.

I bumped into the inventor of emojis the other day, his face was a picture.

Retired astronauts are always very down to earth.

Pundamentalist

I like going to the supermarket naked, so when they ask if I've bought my own bags, I can go 'ta da!'

I remember growing up in Birmingham and being so excited to go and see the Spice Girls, and then so disappointed to find out they weren't really astronauts.

People said I wasn't qualified to teach an assertiveness training course, but I haven't had any complaints so far.

I used to be a mobile hairdresser but that didn't work out, as not enough people had hairy phones.

Gary Delaney

I was named after my dad, and that's because I'm a lot younger than him.

My neighbour's pregnant at the moment. I asked if she knew what the sex was, and she thinks it was probably doggy.

If you're drowning and your life flashes before your eyes, pay close attention to the bit about swimming lessons.

Everyone at my handwriting class is single and male. It's a great place to meet illegible bachelors.

Bad impressionists don't get enough recognition.

Pundamentalist

Apparently Michael Flatley's new show is being
rejigged.

I found my male G-spot recently. Well actually
it was the customs officer who found it.
I just bought him dinner.

Some people say you should punch psychics,
some people say you shouldn't punch psychics,
but I always try to strike a happy medium.

Old MacDonald had Tourette's, ee I ee I, cunt.

'I'm not normally late for my maths lessons,'
he hastened to add.

Gary Delaney

I used to teach origami, but there was just too much paperwork.

My grandad spent his whole life drying out coconuts, which is pointless, but you have to admire his desiccation.

I found some old sex cheques my wife had once given me for my birthday, so I tried to cash them in, but unfortunately nowadays it's all contactless.

Darth Vader was played by the Green Cross Code man, but his voice was replaced by James Earl Jones, when he tried to sneak in the line 'Stop, Luke, and listen!'

Pundamentalist

I went on a course to learn how to complain properly, and it was so good I got my money back.

Apparently the urine in a pub toilet contains as many as 27 different types of peanut.

Paedophile priests? Holy fuck!

Does anyone know any remote Antarctic bases where I can take over the life forms one by one? It's for a Thing.

The hardest part of being a marathon runner in Wales must be keeping up with the Joneses.

Gary Delaney

I was upset at people in the office stealing my highlighter pens, but now I'm just going to draw a line under things.

The inventor of optics has died. I hope you'll all join me in raising a glass to him.

I'm sad to see my biography of Josef Fritzl hasn't made the best cellar lists.

It was only after I shot the fifth zombie that I started to wonder why they were all carrying bags of sweets and ringing my doorbell.

The more I learn about Russian dolls, the more I find there is to learn about Russian dolls.

Pundamentalist

People have told me I've got a Messiah complex, but that's OK, I forgive them.

I used to be terrible at collecting money for charity, and I still am, so no change there.

I used to be a librarian spy, but I can't talk about it, as it was all very hush hush.

My wife's very happy that we've got a new sit on lawnmower. He's called Colin.

Plastic surgeons can now give you a second penis. I'm tempted but worried it might make me a bit too cocky.

The first time a woman saw my penis she called me a freak, which is unfair, because the other one's normal.

I was watching TV, the announcer said there's a documentary about the clitoris on the red button but I couldn't find it.

I had a stressful journey getting here today, all the way here this lorry driver was right up my arse, but it was nice of him to give me a lift.

Times are hard at the minute for people on disability benefit aren't they? I've got a friend who's a dwarf, and he's struggling to put food on the table.

Pundamentalist

During an interview recently the reporter asked if I minded her using a recorder. I said that was fine, and then she started playing Three Blind Mice.

As a young man I used to buy class A drugs, as it made them so much easier to teach.

I said to the travel agent, 'I'm looking for a relaxing holiday in Romania.'
He said, 'Bucharest?'
I said, 'I'm trying to.'

You've got to look after your health as you get older. The other day I did a poo and noticed there was a little blood in it. I said, 'Oi Bruv, get out of me toilet, innit!'

Agent Orange was so named to avoid it ever being mentioned in war poetry.

I like to give a percentage of my earnings to charity, and also other strippers.

I went round Grandad's to walk his dog. As I was leaving the house he said, 'Don't forget poo bags.' I said, 'Alright, Gran, you can come as well.'

I took four E's last night. That was a tough hand at Scrabble.

I rang up Gamblers Anonymous about my fruit machine addiction, and they asked me to hold.

Do I love the conga? Why yes! In fact I come from a long line of conga lovers.

Pundamentalist

People said I was ridiculous to make a poo emoji
hat, but I remain undeterred.

Did I mention that I've got a book coming out?
I don't know why I shoved it up there in the
first place.

I watched the director's cut of a porn film. At the
end he actually fixes the washing machine.

Strange kids have been screaming and knocking
on my door all evening, but no matter how loud
they get, I'm not letting them out.

I've just stolen a load of inflatable mattresses,
so now I'm going to have to lilo for a while.

The sequel to Groundhog Day is Groundhog Day.

When I was little, my grandad said that he could see a lot of himself in me, which is why he's in prison now.

A ventriloquist has been arrested after his doll was found at the scene of a murder. The police believe he may have had a hand in it.

Just found out I've been placed on an MI5 watch list, so now I'm really looking forward to receiving my MI5 watch.

Ironically the word Cyclops doesn't even have one I.

Pundamentalist

I'm terrible at metaphors. To me they're like a big shoe.

However good a baker you are, you've never had as many Hollywood handshakes as Paul Hollywood's penis.

I should never have tried to bluff it as an HGV driver. I've just been asked to back my lorry up and now I can't even find the USB port.

Come on, orange juice, you're a breakfast drink! You've got to patch things up with toothpaste.

My dad put his blood, sweat and tears into everything he did, which is why his restaurant was shut down.

Gary Delaney

It's been a good week for me. On Monday I met
one of my heroes, Craig David. On Tuesday we went
for a drink, so I avoided him on Wednesday.

I don't think cat food should be made from beef
or tuna. It should only be made from things cats
actually eat in the wild like birds, or mice, or dead
pensioners.

I passed my driving test with no major faults.
I did get four minors, but luckily I didn't hit
any adults.

The hardest thing about living in Mexico is if I
ever want to wave to someone, I need another
50,000 people to help.

Pundamentalist

I killed a spider with a shoe earlier. I don't know how he lost the other seven.

Apparently you're supposed to eat chocolate digestives upside down, but when I tried it all the blood ran to my head, and I passed out.

Every selfie I've ever taken is also a portrait of a confused middle aged man trying to figure out which button to press on his phone.

Not a lot of people know this but I used to be an amazing swimmer and then I met an egg.

People who throw themselves off tall buildings have a fatal floor in their plan.

The inventor of Magic Eye pictures is getting a divorce. Apparently his wife was seeing someone behind his back. Still, it's what he would've wanted.

I tell you what makes my blood boil: faulty spacesuits.

People don't like me reading over their shoulder on trains, which is ridiculous as I'm not even that loud and I do ALL the voices.

With the benefit of hindsight, 'Sexy Fenders' was not a good name for a guitar shop.

Pundamentalist

My nephew's upset because he didn't get the
A levels he wanted, so I told him that on my
results day I got 3 Es, and took them all to celebrate
getting into a really good university.

Suggs just asked me what my preferred pronouns
are. Honestly it's Madness gone politically correct.

Red wine and fish certainly don't mix, in fact
mine died.

I thought I was being stopped by a charity mugger,
but it turned out to be an actual mugger, which
worked out cheaper in the long run.

My grandad loved tickling the ivories, but sadly he can't do it anymore, since he got trampled by an elephant.

ENGLISH LESSON'S – Half price!

You shouldn't have a go at fat kids. They've got enough on their plates already.

I've just bought the dictionary as an audiobook, which says it all really.

There are too many perverts in the park nowadays, I walked through earlier and literally everyone kept staring at my erection.

Pundamentalist

I tried to find out the gestation period for
pachyderms, but no one wanted to talk about the
elephant in the womb.

I'll never forget the time someone threw a dart
at me, because some things just stick in your head
don't they?

My brother always used to give me dead legs,
because he was older than me, and worked at the
mortuary.

I just took my car in for a service, and ran over
the priest.

I bought a packet of breath mints. On the side
it said, 'Best before date'. I thought 'Good idea'.

Gary Delaney

Can anyone tell me what FOMO stands for?
Everyone else seems to know.

My wife says the man next door has buns of steel,
as if my masculinity is going to be threatened by
someone who can't even bake properly.

Given how much my phone thinks I'm trying to
write 'ducking', Apple must think we still have a
pretty serious problem with witches.

I'm beginning to think my chiropractor is just
manipulating me.

I bought my nephew a caterpillar cake without
checking the best before date, so now he's got
a butterfly cake.

Pundamentalist

I'd just like to say that rumours I am the owner of the world's biggest bouncy castle have been blown up out of all proportion.

People say using your children's names as passwords isn't secure, but I don't agree, and nor do my kids Chr1s_£!! and little J0hnn1E*%9c.

Grandad always used to talk about D-Day.
He didn't fight in the war, he just had a terrible stutter.

I asked the chemist for some cream for my bottom rash. She said, 'Cutaneous?' I said, 'Thanks very much.'

I had to tell my son he was adopted. He isn't, but he should've tidied his room.

Gary Delaney

I had an interview to be a pilot with RyanAir. They asked, 'Where do you see yourself in 5 years time?' I said, '80 miles away from where I said I was going', and they gave me the job.

I used to be a terrible name dropper, but I tell you who cured me of that, Jonathan Ross.

I've just written my first joke about tantric sex, it's been a long time coming.

My oldest brother is a real estate agent, whereas my younger brother only pretends to be an estate agent.

I have zero tolerance for drugs, which means I do get high very easily.

Pundamentalist

The hardest thing most of us ever have to do
is bury our parents, but what makes it easier is
hitting them with a shovel first.

Never tell a girl with OCD she scrubs up well.

I thought Disney World's fancy dress shop would
be impressive, but it was just a Micky Mouse outfit.

I don't like it when you go to the trouble of writing
someone a letter, they don't bother to reply, and
you end up having to keep the hostage.

A friend of mine likes to boast that he can suck his
own penis. Honestly he's so full of himself.

Gary Delaney

If there was ever a competition for popping
a cap in yo' ass, I'd be the first to throw my hat
into the ring.

Shout out to all the non-fiction authors.
Keeping it real.

Someone told me I was being crabby, so I pinched
him, and walked off sideways.

I'm not saying I'm bored but I've just taken a
laxative and an Imodium to see which one's
fastest.

Bit nervous about doing my first ever gig for
nudists this weekend, but it's alright, I'll just
imagine them wearing clothes.

Pundamentalist

I used to keep carrier pigeons, but now I'm much more environmentally aware, so I've got a pigeon for life.

Ariane Grande is actually only 5 foot 3, so clearly her parents named her using the Starbucks naming system.

I've never been one for putting labels on people, which is why I lost my job at the mortuary.

First session at night school didn't go well, I couldn't even get my lance through the door and it didn't seem like anyone else had really made the effort.

Can circumcisions be carried out at any age, or is there a cut-off date?

Dieting is hard, but I heard black clothes can be very slimming, so now every day I eat two shirts.

Words can't express how good I think my creative writing tutor is.

I met a beautiful women, and we swapped phone numbers, so now all the creepy guys call me instead.

I ordered a mail-order bride, but I was out when she was delivered, so now she's married to my next door neighbour.

I remember one time the Headmaster gave a Special Assembly on ecstasy. We knew something was up when he started dancing to the hymns.

If you do what you love, you'll never work a day in your life, especially if what you love is heroin.

DIY tailoring? Suit yourself.

My wife complained so much about me not fixing the toilet seat that eventually I got a brand new one, and she doesn't care about the toilet seat.

I used to go out with a Yorkshire girl who affectionally called me 'Tintin', because that was what she always said during sex.

A ship full of sailors with lisps was torpedoed by a mystery submarine. Who'd have thunk it?

Apparently putting someone to sleep isn't the same as putting them to bed, and now I'm no longer allowed to work as a vet or a babysitter.

Today is a good day. Not only have I been found not guilty of cruelty to animals, but I've got a new dog to boot.

It turns out that one of my ancestors was Arabian, lived in a lamp, and granted people three wishes. It's amazing what you can find out from a genieology test.

People who are interested in flower pressing should take a leaf out of my book.

Pundamentalist

Why is it that every time they put a new bench in
the park, an old person has to die?

A friend of mine had a penis extension, now his
house looks really stupid.

Ivory hunters. Tsk Tsk!

Breaking News: Archaeologists digging at the site
of Shakespeare's house have uncovered thousands
of monkey skeletons.

They told the inventor of alphabetti spaghetti
it would never work, but he made them eat
their words.

Gary Delaney

I made a papier mâché boob out of newspaper, because I think it's important to keep abreast of current events.

Grandad's in a home now. Amazing, isn't it?
83 years old and he's still a burglar.

Turns up for roast battle
Opponent gets out sheets of scribbled paper, all full of devastating rhyming insults
I look down sadly at my baking tray of chicken, potatoes and vegetables

I used to have a phobia that I was being followed by a clown, but now I can look back and laugh.

My girlfriend says I'm too suspicious. Well she doesn't say it, but she thinks it.

Great news that they're finally outlawing puppy farming. There's no sight more heartbreaking than a baby spaniel desperately struggling to drive a tractor.

My nan still only has a black and white TV, but she didn't even realise until recently, as all she ever watches is interracial porn.

My grandad was killed fighting Germans on the beaches of Normandy, and since then Grandma has refused to go on another package holiday.

One time there was a fire at a voodoo doll factory
and 10,000 people died.

If I had a motto I think it'd be, Je Ne Regrette Rien,
although I don't know what that means, as I
mucked about in French lessons, and I wish
I hadn't now.

'I rang you but I couldn't get through.'

'What number did you call me on?'

'X, IV, X, C, I, III, L, M, X, VII.'

'Sorry, that's an old number.'

People have told me I'm not very good at
comebacks, but I say to them, 'No, YOU'RE not
very good at comebacks.'

Pundamentalist

My nan used to suck off Americans for chocolate
and stockings, and then there was a war.

One night I wished a diabetic friend sweet dreams
and they ended up in a coma.

My kid loves the new Star Wars films and said
he'd love to see BB8 in real life, so I drove him to
Blackburn.

I've just been to Jamie Oliver's website and it asked
me to accept cookies. Hypocrite!

Give a man a fish and you feed him for a day.
Teach him to fish, and you feed him for a lifetime.
Assuming he lives by an abundant source of fish,
yet has somehow never heard of fishing.

Gary Delaney

I'm not saying I was an unpopular child, but I had an imaginary acquaintance.

People say if you wank too much you'll end with forearms like Popeye, which is ridiculous, as he only has two arms.

Why did pirates have parrots for pets? If you have a job that's highly illegal, surely the last thing you want is something that repeats word for word everything you've ever done.

Get free portraits of loved ones by simply reporting them for serious crimes and describing them to police sketch artists.

Pundamentalist

My brother's through to Judges' Houses on
X Factor. He can't sing to save his life, but he's
a great burglar.

Of course I can't afford a voice activated car, it goes
without saying.

One time I accidentally played YMCA at the
Dyslexics' disco. It was mayhem.

There was an old man, from Limerick who wanted,
to be a haiku.

I've just put some moisturiser on. Let that sink in
for a moment.

Gary Delaney

A friend of mine made a fortune on the Grand National this year, because he owns a glue factory and a kebab shop.

The guy next to me at work used to watch porn all day. I'm just glad he didn't begin to rub off on me.

My grandad was a famous spy in World War Two, which is how he got caught.

I once met a sexy Welsh girl at a party. She said, 'Why don't you come back to mine?' So I did, and for the next 20 years I had to work down a mine.

Pundamentalist

It's a sad fact that many comics were actually comedy fans when they were young, and so the cycle continues and the amused becomes the amuser.

Have you had an accident at work? Then just pop to the toilet when no one's looking and change your pants.

Some people say Christopher Lee never played any iconic roles, but they're wrong on at least two Counts.

When it comes to pastry earmuffs I'm a bit of a pioneer.

Sad news. I've just heard that the inventor of predictive text is I'll. Hopefully hell get we'll soon.

Someone once told me I was the second least inquisitive man in the world, and I said, 'Well, that's good then'.

I've just been cast as Oliver Twist, who could ask for more?

I recently entered a competition to see who's gained the most weight and lost the most hair. Obviously it wasn't called that, it was advertised as a 'School Reunion'.

Pundamentalist

I did terribly in the reverse parking on my driving test, but luckily I passed anyway and I haven't looked back since.

It takes years of training to be a physiotherapist, so you do have to exercise patience.

If your rice is too soggy just leave it overnight in a bowl of mobile phones.

The saddest thing about Edward Scissorhands was that he loved to run.

I caught my girlfriend playing with her phone during sex, which I think is rude, especially as it was a landline.

I hired a landscape gardener, but he said he couldn't help because my garden was portrait.

I've just bought Spider-Man pyjamas. I hope he likes them.

I've got a book out at the moment. I don't want to get carried away though, it's got to go back in two weeks.

I just trod on a landmine. That's me all over.

I bet the inventor of autocorrect is a massive walker.

Pundamentalist

Damn girl, are you M C Escher? Because you draw stares.

I, O, I, O, it's off to work as a binary programmer I go.

How many lightbulbs does it take to change a person? – SAD Research Centre

The other day I deleted internet history and now no one remembers who Tim Berners-Lee is.

I got into a fight with my yoga instructor and she walked out mid-lesson, which left me in a very awkward position.

Gary Delaney

I tried a bit of nude painting today. It went really well, and now everyone says my front door looks lovely.

I've just asked the man from Del Monte who his favourite prog rock band is.

This new rowing machine really works! We're already bickering over how much it cost and how long until it gets shoved in the loft.

I'm thinking of wearing a really tight white t-shirt but I'm not sure I could pull it off.

Magnum 3.14159

Pundamentalist

My favourite thing to see at the zoo is all the divorced dads.

Say what you like about waiters, but I think they bring a lot to the table.

If the towns of Towcester and Bath were closer together that'd be really dangerous.

This diet was hard at first but now I'm really starting to find my feet.

To be honest I didn't really understand the story of 'The Emperor's New Clothes' but everyone else did, so I pretended I did too.

Gary Delaney

Bishop: 'Has anyone seen my pointy hat?'

Vicar: 'Mitre?'

Bishop: 'Don't piss about, mate. Have you seen it or not?'

I think my biggest USB is that I don't really care about using the correct acronyms.

If you pay Charles M. Schulz you get Peanuts.

My new boss told me he expects me to be on call 24/7 but I don't really mind as July 24th is ages away.

If I had a pound for every time I've taken a supermarket trolley back . . .

My new book on poltergeists is literally flying off the shelves.

I came second in a Fidel Castro look-alike competition. Close, but no cigar.

'I wonder what's in that field?'

'Herd of cows?'

'Yes.'

'Well it's them'.

I worry that when James Dyson dies he'll leave behind a power vacuum.

Ignoring my advice, a friend of mine paid £2000 for a 'miracle cure' for his speech impediment. At least he can't say I didn't warn him.

People say that if you can make a woman laugh it's easier to get her into bed, but I've always found it's the other way round.

I think my biggest vice is probably buying over-sized DIY equipment.

Statisticians can pretend to be nice in the short term but in the long run they always revert to mean.

I thought sea cows were extinct, but it turns out they're doing quite well, and that's restored my faith in huge manatees.

Pundamentalist

The greatest trick the Breville ever pulled was convincing people they'd make toasted sandwiches for more than a day.

I've been to see a therapist about my compulsive shoplifting of Apple products. He told me to keep taking the tablets.

Correlation does not imply causality, but the more I say things like that the less people want to talk to me.

I don't much fancy tobogganing but I would do it if pushed.

This dating app is useless. Everyone I meet seems to be just another creepy talking chocolate egg. That's the last time I use Kinder.

Fun idea: Dress up as the Prophet Mohammed, then sit in front of the caricaturists in Leicester square and watch them shit themselves.

If the devil ever finds out I've stolen his favourite wig there'll be hell toupee.

I'm a big fan of home cooking or, as the police insisted on calling it, arson.

Obviously I'm disappointed that I was refused planning permission to build a house on this plot of land, but I'm not going to dwell on it.

I don't think I'll ever suddenly inherit millions of pounds, not with the best will in the world.

My plan for an Al Pacino impressions competition seems to have caused a bit of a hoo-ha.

The Easter story is proof God worked in IT Support. 'Have you tried turning him off then on again?'

A potato wrapped in foil makes an ideal Easter egg for a vegan child.

There are two types of people who don't like Easter. Type 1 People on diets and Type 2 Diabetics.

Gary Delaney

You have to feel sorry for Jesus, not only
was he crucified, but right at the start of the
four day weekend.

I've just found a DVD hidden amongst my
Easter eggs.

I've given up making innuendos for Lent, but
it's getting really hard now and I'm not sure if
I can pull it off.

At least if I make an Easter joke today and it dies,
I can just bring it back on Sunday and everyone
will think it's brilliant.

I bought a special alarm clock for politicians.
It's got a schmooze button, and two faces.

Pundamentalist

The hippocampus is the part of the brain I use
to imagine what it would look like if hippos went
to university.

Recreate the excitement of Russian Roulette
by putting a lullaby on your iPod and having it
on shuffle whilst driving.

Last night I got absolutely shit-faced.
Moral of the story?
Never buy a cheap glass coffee table.

I've just got my A level results. AAA!
Sorry, not A level results, batteries.

The weird thing about doing Schrödinger's Cat
jokes is you can never tell if they've died.

Gary Delaney

I'm pleased to see that the first issue of
'Constipation Monthly' magazine comes with
a free ring binder.

I recently took my naval exams. I got seven Cs.

As my old Vicar always used to say, making a
poster is a lot like christening a fat child – you need
a bigger font.

Warning: If your birthday is on Valentine's Day
then the postman probably thinks you're a slag.

My brother just admitted that he broke my
favourite lamp. I'm not sure I'll be able look at him
in the same light ever again.

Pundamentalist

Quick child maintenance question. Is it every 10,000 or 15,000 miles?

I had a really vivid dream the council was taking back my allotment from me. For a moment I thought I was losing the plot.

It's very hard to write a reasonable sounding email complaining that the caps lock key on your new computer is broken.

Bad news, there's been a flood at the silica gel factory. No wait, hang on, it's fine.

Having just found out what MILF means I'm becoming increasingly concerned about '80s sitcom ALF.

Gary Delaney

If I ever find the guy who messed up my
limb transplants, I'm going to kill him with
my bear hands.

I'm thinking of buying some Stephen King
audiobooks, but I've heard a few horror stories.

The worst thing about living next door to
MC Hammer is the constant DIY noise. I shouted
'Stop!' but if anything that made it worse.

If Bing Crosby was great, imagine how good
Google Crosby would have been.

I fixed Aretha Franklin's computer. It would appear
sisters are not doing IT for themselves.

Pundamentalist

Pilot whales strand themselves on beaches as
they've given up hope of ever getting a full series.

Not a good start to my first day in mine clearance.
Let's just say it took me a while to find my feet.

In the '80s my nickname was 'Drugs', because
when I asked girls out, they'd just say 'No'.

I just asked Billy Bunter if he was pregnant.
Massive schoolboy error.

I filed an exclusive news story about the world's
most generous ice cream man.
What a scoop!

'What do we want?'

'Time travel.'

'When do we want it?'

'Doesn't matter.'

I've never done any sheep worrying, but I once made a lamb stew.

The Secret Millionaire's Shortbread – a millionaire helps out a hard-pressed charity but what they don't know is he's also hidden some shortbread.

The trouble with learning how to play the violin is that it's a bit fiddly.

A great way to improve the taste of iced tea is to heat it up and add milk.

Pundamentalist

Work out your real name by taking what people call you and adding your parents' surname.

There's nothing more embarrassing than accidentally calling a teacher mum, especially during sex.

A lamppost near me has gone missing so I've sellotaped posters to all the local cats.

I thought *Orange Is the New Black* was a documentary about what happened when Trump replaced Obama.

A man ran up to me shouting, 'Big hole in the ground full of water, big hole in the ground full of water', but at least he means well.

Gary Delaney

Just ahead of every greyhound bus is a smaller, faster rabbit bus.

My girlfriend left me for Professor Brian Cox. She said she needed more space.

My psychiatrist keeps shouting that he's fallen into a well, but I think it's really just a cry for help.

I had a scary moment on the train earlier. I thought someone had coughed on the back of my neck, but luckily it was only spunk.

I used to really fancy a quantum physicist, but sometimes it was like she didn't even know I existed.

Pundamentalist

My uncle hung himself at a Mexican birthday party.
It was pretty messy.

I took out an endowment mortgage. If I don't
keep up the repayments, they cut my cock off.

Stick insects have sex very carefully in case of fire.

As a child I was forced to exercise by my father,
who in turn was forced to exercise by his father.
I only hope that I can break the cycle.

I ordered a load of bubble wrap just to see what
it's delivered in.

I was at the bookshop and the conspiracy theory section was roped off.

I can't believe that's just a coincidence.

Walt Disney always swore he'd never allow Mickey Mouse to be used for tacky merchandising.

'Not on my watch.'

I've just been on a course on sexual harassment in the workplace and I think I'm getting really good at it.

In America, 'Pride' comes just before Autumn.

I asked my therapist never to tell anyone about my Oedipus complex. He said, 'Sure, mum's the word.'

Pundamentalist

A minicab driver and a microbiologist, but who's
the smallest?

Thinking of investing my life savings in a
company that makes wedding cakes, but I'm
worried it'll all end in tiers.

I think if I could have just one superpower
it'd be China.

I met a man who reminded me of my dad.
He came up to me and said, 'Don't forget your dad.'

If they were ever looking for volunteers to help at
Customs, I'd be the first to put my hand up.

Gary Delaney

When people tell me I'm too anal, I just give them a wry smile, and add their name to my spreadsheet.

I joined Amnesty International because they had a special offer on: buy one set one free.

A dwarf just arrived for my birthday, which was actually last week. Too little, too late.

I'm in a same sex relationship.
After ten years the sex is always the same.

One time I went coarse fishing and caught three fucking fish.

Pundamentalist

I rang up a sex line. The woman said, 'I'll do anything you want.'

I said, 'OK, reverse the charges.'

Great Uncle Bulgaria's got Alzheimer's. It's so sad, he doesn't even remember he's a Womble.

The 300th rule of OCD club is . . .

Choirboys refer to singing from the same hymn sheet as 'making sure they all agree on corporate objectives'.

My dad had a chicken farm, rather than do it himself.

Nowadays, Botox is nothing to be frowned upon.

Vanilla Ice fans, they get a bad rap.

I accidentally let slip to a French boy that his dad wasn't his real dad. So that was a faux pas.

Just re-reading 'Peter Pan'. It never gets old.

I suffered from premature ejaculation, but I was too shy, too embarrassed to talk about it.
Eventually I screwed up the courage to go and see my doctor, showed her my penis and said,
'I'm worried I might be a bit premature.'
She said, 'You certainly are, I'm the receptionist.'

Pundamentalist

It's a good job Hitler killed himself, he'd only have got more right-wing as he got older.

People who believe in homeopathy are OK in small doses.

I'm thinking of having a DIY sex change but I'm not sure I can pull it off.

I lost three stone on the Adam Ant diet, and it's so easy. 'Don't chew ever, don't chew ever . . .'

A warning to the man who stole my owl costume, I'd be looking over my shoulder if I was you.

Gary Delaney

I'm trying to give up eating cold turkey, but how?
I reckon gradually.

I don't really like lip readers, but I'd never say that
to their face.

It must be hard getting dumped by someone with
Multiple Personality Disorder. 'It's not you, it's us.'

I've been having some trouble with my server
today, he still refuses to bring me my slippers.

My local Domino's Pizza has burnt down, and now
I fear for the rest of them.

Pundamentalist

Sad news: apparently the Michelin Man has retyred.

Fun idea: Not got kids? Hire a babysitter anyway, say your kid is asleep upstairs and not to be woken. On your return ask where your child is.

Everyone says 50 is the new 40, but I got 3 points and a £100 fine.

I always vowed I'd never molest my pet lions, but eventually I swallowed my pride.

I read a book on cocaine addiction, after the first few lines I was hooked.

This Spinal Tap clock is rubbish, it only goes up to eleven.

I'm quite a sensitive man. I don't mind being held after sex, it's only when they press charges it gets tricky.

When I crossed the picket line at the National Eczema Society they all shouted 'Scab.'
So I said, 'Well, you shouldn't picket.'

I applied for a job. They said send in your CV, and I loved that car.

Tiger Woods . . . that was no place for a picnic.

Pundamentalist

I wrote a book on penguins. Paper would have been easier.

I passed a milestone earlier today. I shouldn't have eaten it really.

I learned about this great diet from a Saudi Arabian cannibal. It was so easy. You just have a Sheikh for breakfast . . .

I went out with a Lady-in-waiting which is a posh way of saying pre-op transsexual.

I went out with a little pink mouse who lived on the moon. We split up, and only then did I realise that I'd dropped a Clanger.

Mirror, mirror on the wall who's the fairest of
them all? It's the albino girl.

We buried my cousin this week, but at least he died
doing what he loved. Heroin.

Nan would always send us texts saying please
come round, my arthritis is getting worse.
But eventually they stopped. So presumably it
got better.

It's thanks to the efforts of men like my grandad
that we don't speak German today, because he
single handedly killed eleven language teachers.

Pundamentalist

The recession's been affecting everyone. My
brother's tightening his belt a lot at the moment,
but then he is a heroin addict.

I used to run a brickyard in Liverpool, but I came in
one morning and it was up on wheels.

A friend of mine can't help shouting out the
names of different parts of castles. He's got Turret's
syndrome.

Humans and dolphins are the only two species
to have sex for pleasure, which is OK if you
don't mind the clicky noises.

I used to go out with a biologist, but I found out
she'd been faking her organisms.

Gary Delaney

The Tower of Pisa is probably the most famous listed building.

Just watched Edward Scissorhands. I thought it was better than Edward Paperhands but not as good as Edward Stonehands.

I've got a solution to the growing problem of obesity in schoolchildren, bring back bullying.

People who shoplift dictionaries have got a way with words.

Does anyone know what ASMR is?
I've only heard whispers.

Pundamentalist

My grandparents have been happily married for 50 years so I asked them what their secret was. His was that you should never go to bed on an argument, whereas she said she'd once sucked off his brother.

There's a lot of discussion amongst historians over whether Shakespeare died of Tuberculosis. TB or not TB? That is the question.

Being an organ donor can be disheartening.

I stood up at a Jean-Michel Jarre concert and now I don't need to wear glasses anymore.

Gary Delaney

People are more aware of mental health nowadays.
Did you know that at some point more than
3 people out of every 2 will suffer from Multiple
Personality Disorder?

I'm feeling pretty positive today. Just this morning
my dry cleaner said to me, 'You're in charge.'
I said, 'Thanks, mate.' He said, 'No, it's an extra
ten pounds to clean these trousers. Urine charge.'

My little brother won a goldfish at the fairground,
and the very next morning we found him floating
in the pond dead. So I had to look after the fish.

Being in a wheelchair never stopped my little
brother from misbehaving, in fact he was often to
be found sitting on the naughty ramp.

Pundamentalist

Sometimes I say harsh things about them on stage but I do love my little family. We've actually got two beautiful children, and another one.

I love getting pampered at the weekend, although it can be hard getting nappies in my size.

Find out your porn star name by embarking on an exciting new career in porn.

Sometimes I like to go to the Library and hide the Where's Wally books.

My brother used to say, 'What doesn't kill you makes you stronger', then he started taking steroids and died.

My girlfriend's started sleep-talking, which can be really off-putting during sex.

My girlfriend was shocked the first time I sent her a dick pic. But not as much as I was when she sent me one.

I fell out with my mum a long time ago.
Sorry, I fell out of my mum a long time ago.

There's only one thing I don't like about Halloween, which is.

Last Halloween I was arrested for making anyone dressed as Dracula give me piggybacks. I was found guilty on four counts.

Pundamentalist

My uncle's motto was 'There's always one prick in a bunch of roses', and that's why he lost his job as a florist.

Wondering who sent you a card on Valentine's Day? Good. Wondering who sent you a card on Father's Day? Bad.

Our Lord Jesus spent 40 days and nights fasting in the desert, as he was embarrassed about how many pancakes he'd eaten.

While my wife is at her remedial maths class, I'm having an affair with her sister. I just hope she never puts two and two together.

Gary Delaney

The tensest crowd I've ever seen was at the funeral of the man who invented the Jack-in-the-box.

I saw a man with Tourette's playing a fruit machine, nudge, nudge, wink, wink.

Never buy cheap lube. It'll only end in tears.

People who always go on about how good they are at yoga can go fuck themselves.

I accidentally kicked my dog earlier and it bit me on the bollocks. My mate said, 'It's karma.' I said, 'No, if anything it's even more angry.'

Pundamentalist

I bought a Father's Day card in Croydon and it just said Guess Who?

I had a vindaloo last night, and today my arse really stings. I couldn't afford to pay the bill, and the chef bummed me.

I met a rather large woman who said she was from Wales, which I presume she meant in evolutionary terms.

I thought Snapchat was a support group for people with brittle bone disease.

If a jellyfish stings you you're supposed to piss on it, which presumably is to teach it a lesson.

Gary Delaney

I went on a lads' holiday to Thailand and slept with a Ladyboy. My friends said, 'Couldn't you see her Adam's Apple?', I said, 'Not under that beard'.

Old people aren't nosy, the real reason they poke their heads through curtains all the time is they're practising for being cremated.

I remember as a teenager having an awkward conversation with Dad about sex, and I had to explain I just didn't see him that way.

My favourite TV programme is *The Walking Dead*, or as it's more commonly known, *Songs of Praise*.

Pundamentalist

I recently won a competition to win a month's supply of free milk. Well I say that, the old lady next door died.

These noise cancelling headphones work so well in the quiet carriage. So far I've used them to strangle three people.

More Americans are killed by shootings than by fire, and that's because in America if you shout 'Fire!', someone will shoot you.

My girlfriend's been thinking about getting a stud on her tongue. Apparently he's called Mark.

I tried emailing the doctor to get some laxatives, but unfortunately it got stuck in my out box.

I had a small part in a porn film once, which is why I wasn't very good at that job.

My vicar said the helium I gave him was the best he's ever inhaled before a service. High praise indeed.

I don't think Botox is as expensive as people say. When they're given the bill they never look surprised.

I was on holiday in Cornwall and I asked this old man where the nearest police station was. He laughed and said there wasn't one for 20 miles. I said, 'Well in that case, give me your wallet.'

Pundamentalist

It turns out I've been doing entirely the wrong sort of training for the Ironman challenge, but on the plus side my shirts look lovely.

A great way to get over being nervous about a new partner seeing you naked for the first time is just to imagine them public speaking.

My Liverpudlian cousin did really well in his Scouser exams, he got an A, A, A, and a calm down.

When I failed my seismology exam I just wanted the ground to open up and swallow me, but we all know that's impossible.

If I was to take my favourite parts of all the most beautiful women in the world, and mix them all together, then I'd have a big pile of tits.

In the jungle animals find out if they're pregnant by weeing on a stick insect.

The young couple next door to me have recently made a sex tape, I mean obviously they don't know that yet.

Last time I was here a girl asked me for sex. I had to disappoint her. We had sex.

I was on a long drive and I stopped for a piss at a Little Chef, but unfortunately he ducked at the last second so I only splashed his hat.

Pundamentalist

I used to go out with a parachutist with IBS but
she shat on me from a great height.

I've currently got a stalker, but you probably can't
tell in these trousers.

My grief counsellor died recently but luckily
he was so good I didn't give a shit.

The other day I was doing the hoovering in my
pants and I thought to myself, how do my bollocks
get this dusty?

I think the hardest part of making skimmed milk
must be throwing the cows across the lake.

Of course, some of the cows only make it half-way
across the lake . . .

I used to be a fortune teller but all I ever predicted was really cold winters. It turned out the crystal ball shop had sold me a snow globe.

I think it's sad the word legend has been devalued from pulling a sword from a stone to unexpectedly returning with crisps.

I tried swimming with dolphins once, but I didn't like it, as I found them very cliquey.

When you get a new car you're paranoid about scratching it. I parked at Asda and when I came out there was a big gash on the bonnet. I said, 'Madam, sit on your own car.'

Pundamentalist

I tell you what always catches my eye, short people
with umbrellas.

I took a poll recently and 100% of people were
quite annoyed that their tent had fallen down.

We've got two kids, Jane and Emma, sadly they
do both get bullied at school. I can't make it stop
but I can help them learn how to rise above it,
so the other day I said to them, 'Look, boys . . .'

My manager said that if I was to tour America
I could double the size of my audience.
It would still be the same number of people . . .

I put on a lot of weight so I rang up Weight Watchers. I said, 'It's an emergency can you send somebody round?', and they said, 'Yes we can we've got loads of them.'

I was actually thrown out of Weight Watchers for making sarcastic comments at the weekly weigh in. As you can imagine I accepted the decision with huge grace, because they threw her out as well.

I've got two lawyers working for me at the minute, one's pro-bono and the other thinks he's a right pretentious twat.

Women can be very insecure about their appearance. I was once going out with this very very beautiful Thai girl who constantly wanted reassurance about the size of her penis.

Pundamentalist

I like to think I'm a bit like Superman. For example the other day I changed in a phone box from a man who really needed a wee to a man who's just had a wee.

It's been a tough week. I bought myself a memory foam mattress and now it's trying to blackmail me.

I was in a fancy lingerie shop and I said, 'Are these knickers satin?' He said, 'No they're new.'

Why is it that when women go to the toilet in pairs no one minds but when I did it, I got thrown out of the greengrocer's?

People always describe Cliff Richard as asexual, but I'd also add B) gay.

I went on a barging holiday. I haven't got a boat,
I just kept pushing people into canals.

The doctor told me to lose some weight. I said,
'How?' He said, 'Don't eat anything fatty.' I said,
'What, pies, chips, that sort of thing?' He said,
'No, just don't eat anything, fatty.'

I don't like to eat anything labelled reformed ham
as I think it's unfair that the pigs are slaughtered
after they've got their lives back on track.

This morning I made a Belgian waffle, in the
afternoon I made a Frenchman talk bollocks.

Pundamentalist

The President of France said this week that English speakers were arrogant in their refusal to learn other languages. At least I think that's what he said. But it all just sounded like haw he haw he haw he haw . . .

I like to annoy my Israeli flatmate, by giving him any post that's just addressed to The Occupier.

Optimists are half full of shit.

My girlfriend recently said that I've got a cock like a donkey. Turns out she meant the smell.

Which does pose the question: how does she know what a donkey's cock smells like?

But at least now I know why she's banned from Blackpool Pleasure Beach.

And why she always called it that.

Gary Delaney

I was in a sex shop and saw a dildo described as nine inches long and realistic. I thought, well which is it?

They always say you'll find the love of your life when you're not really looking, which was true, but by then I'd run her over.

As a family we couldn't decide whether to have Nana buried or cremated, so in the end we let her live.

My grandad went down in history, and on one occasion fingered a girl in geography.

If you're ever being strangled to death why not make the most of it by having a wank?

Pundamentalist

I shouldn't have hired a hipster roofer, now
my whole house is covered in plates.

I think the worst thing about having sex with your
mum would be if you lost your erection she'd say
'Well, where did you last have it?'

Grandma was alcoholic. So, we drank her.

I was woken up last night by the bulimic upstairs
vomiting. So I banged on the ceiling going 'Oi!
Keep it down!'
I know, it's easy to scoff.

I'm so good at playing Operation that I once heard
my wife telling one of her friends that I never even
touch the sides.

Gary Delaney

My grandad's not racist, but his parrot is.

My grandad said he wanted to be cremated and then he died just two days later, because he didn't say when.

I'm hoping to go an entire month without using any euphemisms for masturbation. Touch wood.

I had a pub lunch today. There was a sign saying 'The Chef's Special', so at least that explained the food.

'I took my dog to an auction at a stately home.'
'Tudor Furniture?'
'No, but he pissed against a cabinet.'

Pundamentalist

I went to see my nan yesterday. I said, 'What you been up to?'
She said, 'Weedin' the garden.'
I said, 'Well, at least you didn't shit in it.'

I'm not saying my dad was mean, but he blinded himself just to get a free dog.

Someone's stolen my diary. Oh my days!

Before you joke about victims of landmines
you should try walking a mile in their shoes,
because they don't need them.

Gary Delaney

When answering the security question 'Place of birth?' apparently 'vagina' is not an acceptable answer.

I like to call photos of other people 'someoneelsies'.

I'm not very musical but as a choirboy I was allowed to play on the church organ.
Well I say that, it is was the vicar's cock.

I can give you the leading cause of anaphylactic shock in a nutshell.

It was my girlfriend who suggested we have a long distance relationship. I said, 'But we already live together.' She said, 'Yeah, about that . . .'

Pundamentalist

I took my dog to the groomer's today. He doesn't need a haircut, we just went round my dodgy uncle's.

I had an argument with a sailor over why some dolphins were angry, but it turned out we were talking at cross porpoises.

Does it count as polyamorous if, as well as having a girlfriend, you've also fingered a parrot?

Every year thousands of homeless are tossed on the streets, and it's even worse for the ones who don't get tossed.

Gary Delaney

My next door neighbour's really loud and
obnoxious, so now I know how Canada feels.

I suffered from premature ejaculation which
made me feel selfish and bad for my girlfriend.
Then she suggested I try this special cream that
reduces your sensitivity, and it really worked,
because now I didn't give a fuck about her.

When people die and head towards the light
what they don't realise is they've already been
reincarnated as a moth.

My wife said if I carry on being so pedantic
eventually I'll find I've got less and less friends.
I said, 'No I won't. I'll find I've got fewer and fewer
friends.'

I'd love to compete in the Paralympics but it looks like it costs an arm and a leg.

If someone's killed in a fire do you get a discount on the cremation?

You can't be sent to jail for tax avoidance, which is a shame, as then you'd really find out what it's like for a loophole to be abused.

I saw four armed police officers at the airport this morning. How ridiculous! Where do they get uniforms that fit?

Gary Delaney

If you're caught using mascara in Saudi Arabia do they give you 50 lashes?

People waiting for organ donors. My heart goes out to them.

I used to make my own porn on an Etch A Sketch. I'd spend hours drawing a pair of boobs, and then rub one out.

Yesterday I stopped a kidnapping. I leaned over his little pram and screamed, 'Wake up!'.

Bondage is tricky at first, but it's easier if you've got someone to show you the ropes.

Pundamentalist

Someone just asked me if I was sporty, which is great as I haven't been mistaken for a Spice Girl for ages.

If you think kale and açai berries are superfoods then you're going to lose your shit when you try ice cream.

Apparently Marvin Gaye should now be called Marvin LGBTQ+

Last night I had toad in the hole. He was livid.

Roll on deodorant always sounds like something people used to say before deodorant was invented.

Gary Delaney

A friend of mine tried to commit suicide by
putting a 50 watt bulb up his bottom. I said,
'It's all right mate, don't worry. There's light at
the end of the tunnel.'
Anyway, he brightened up in the end.

I think the worst thing about getting really old
would be going to Dignitas and then forgetting
what you've gone in for.

I went to visit some friends in China. They had
this most incredible drawing on their fridge.
I said, 'That is fantastic. Did your five-year-old
make that?' They said, 'Yes he did, and the
washing machine and dishwasher as well.'

Pundamentalist

A friend of mine got caught trying to shoplift a mobile phone in Saudi Arabia, but luckily it was hands free.

My best friend at college was always known as Claire with an E, because she was a drug dealer.

My grandad always complains about the amount of shit on telly nowadays, but he's the one who throws it.

My nan's been suffering from dementia. She rang me up the other day to say that she'd had waffles for breakfast. When I went to see her, her little dog was gone.

It's never a good idea to have sex with somebody in the workplace, is it? Because then you have to see them every day, it gets awkward. Eventually everybody finds out and then you're no longer allowed to teach.

I'm not saying kids grow up too fast these days, but I've just seen one trying to swipe left on Guess Who?

I was in a queue at the fairground for the 'I Guess Your Weight' stall. Eventually I get to the front. The guy looks at me and goes, 'Well, I'd say that was about 20 minutes.'

Our six-year-old refuses to eat anything other than Alphabetti Spaghetti. Luckily he's dyslexic, so we just buy him normal spaghetti.

Pundamentalist

I was in Wales recently. I went to a tourist attraction called The Devil's Bridge. It got its name from the fact that it's where they used to try witches. They would chuck some poor woman off the bridge, and if she was a witch she'd fly away, whereas if she was innocent she'd fall to her death on the M4.

If anything, finding out that Jimmy Savile was a paedophile made it even worse that he never answered my letters.

All of my favourite '70s Kids TV stars have been done for it, haven't they? Jimmy Savile, Rolf Harris, Stuart Hall. I bet Finger Mouse is shitting himself.

Gary Delaney

A paedophile goes into a florist's.
'I'd like some flowers please.'
'Orchids?'
'No, just the flowers.'

I thought PPI was just something you could get at the swimming baths.

I remember one time at school the teacher asked me to spell schadenfreude, and I couldn't. But he's dead now and I'm not, so I win.

I read a book on Stockholm Syndrome, it started badly but by the end I loved it.

If a man uses too much pornography, eventually it starts to affect his whole attitude towards slags.

Pundamentalist

One time at a party I chucked my car keys into
a big bowl, and everybody just stared at me, and
the trifle was ruined.

Just seen a lovely horse-drawn carriage. I'm
amazed they can even hold a pencil.

Why is it that every time I go to the gym Princess
Diana dies?

I recently lost my thesaurus. I still can't find the
words describe how upset I am.

I was in WHSmith's. I bought a book of 1,000
raffle tickets for £2.50, which is a bargain because
normally they're a pound a strip.
I didn't win.

Gary Delaney

As kids we always enjoyed dipping ginger nuts into a steaming hot cup of tea, but of course nowadays that's called bullying.

Ginger jokes are the last vestiges of racism in comedy. They've started a ginger pride movement to stamp that shit out. They had a march in Hyde Park. Well they were going to but the sun came out.

Panty liners. That was the worst cruise I've ever been on.
Especially the Red Sea.

Recently, I was fingered for a crime, which is quite a harsh punishment.

Pundamentalist

When I was young, I went out with an older woman who taught me that the best way to perform cunnilingus is to use your tongue to trace out the letters of the alphabet. So I learned how to do that and I was pretty pleased with myself, and then she left me for a Chinese guy.

My girlfriend's dog died, so to cheer her up I got her an identical one. She was livid. 'What I'm I going to do with two dead dogs?'

My girlfriend always says my problem is I never follow through on projects. So I shat on her stamp collection.

Gary Delaney

My grandad's trying to keep up with new technology. I got a text off him the other day. 'I've had a stroke and now my head's hanging to one side. Lol.'

I've got a small penis, but it's all right because my girlfriend's an optimist. To her the vagina is always half full.

I went to the supermarket and they had a special on. He collects the trolleys.

I recently went down on my girlfriend without realizing she was having a period. As you can imagine, I was very red in the face.
I felt such a clot.

Pundamentalist

I can't believe my wife only got me a Scrabble set
for my birthday. We shall be having words.

I recently tried twerking. It was a disaster,
and in the end the doctor couldn't even check
my prostate.

I used to work at McDonald's. Mostly flipping
burgers but we also sold fucking chips as well.

Do you think Jesus ever regretted asking
Pontius Pilate to put him up for the weekend?

The boiler broke yesterday and I had to get a man
out, which poses the question what was he doing
in my boiler?

Gary Delaney

I often confuse Americans and Canadians,
by using long words.

Sad news. The inventor of spellcheck has died.
My thoughs are with his family.

In my 20s, I could eat what I liked and always
get away with it. And then I reached my 30s
and people started labelling the food in the
office fridge.

One time I nearly had a threesome with
my girlfriend and my best friend and the only
thing that stopped it happening was they didn't
invite me.

Pundamentalist

My dad has brittle bone disease which meant he struggled to bring us up, especially when it came to smacking us. But at least he really meant it when he said this is going to hurt me more than it's going to hurt you.

My nan always said don't do anything I wouldn't do, which is tricky as that ruled out walking, remembering things, and not being racist.

My daughter's started discovering boys, so that'll teach her to dig up the patio.

My rubber ring says 'not to be used as a life preserver'. It was tough watching that guy drown, but rules are rules.

Our fourth child was called Ivy. And that's because we ran out of names and started using Roman numerals.

When people die and head towards the light, what they don't realise is they've already been reincarnated as a moth.

A man has been found guilty of overusing commas. The judge warned him to expect a very long sentence.

My nan was 112 when she died. Mind you a temperature like that would have killed anyone.

Pundamentalist

A psychic told me I was going to become a grandfather. I said, 'How could you possibly know that?' He said, 'I've got your daughter pregnant.'

So they did a big study, and apparently the least sexy place for a woman to get a tattoo is Croydon.

As a child I was always told that if I touched myself down there God was watching, but it turned out it was just Uncle Peter.

I'm a terrible ventriloquist, if I do say so myself.

Ironically I buy shitloads of Imodium.

Gary Delaney

I've just been asked to bury the world's fattest man,
which is a massive undertaking.

My brother had a drum kit fall on his head and
it led to percussion, but don't worry, it sounds
a lot worse than it actually is.

I rang up the penis enlargement clinic, and they
said, 'What extension do you require?'

There's a fine line between numerators and
denominators.

Sometimes I'm my own harshest critic, and
I'm not even very good at that.

Pundamentalist

I've been attending Gamblers Anonymous for three years whereas my best mate Dave only stuck it out for two and a half. So I won that one.

Grandad died doing what he loved. Being ill.

Is it OK that I start drinking as soon as the kids are at school? Or does that make me a bad teacher?

Opera tenors are always male. I suggested trying a tenor lady, but they said it was taking the piss.

How often have I met the Fugees? One time.

I spent three years at university studying sound engineering. I came out with a 2-1 . . . 2, 1, 2.

I got a ransom note in the post. 'Pay us a million pounds, or you'll never see your child again'. I couldn't believe it. Who still writes letters?

I haven't attended my self-harmers support group for eight weeks now, but I'm not going to beat myself up about it.

'Are you really a member of a rapid response te—'
'Yes.'

Every loch has its quay.

Pundamentalist

I thought restaurants serving everything on slates was bad enough, but apparently now my grandad is getting meals on wheels.

People say I'm too cynical, but they would, wouldn't they?

I loved watching the Star Wars films as a six-year-old boy. The best part was dressing up as a six-year-old.

I used to suffer from schizophrenic delusions and think I was a magazine. That was back when I was Just 17.

Private browsing is mostly used for browsing privates.

Gary Delaney

Sure Covid-19 is bad now, but in the future it will be a boon for bingo callers.

If I could get my pigeons to seize control of the state that would be a real coup.

A friend of mine borrowed all my Tippex, then the next time I saw him he blanked me.

Can someone read some self-help books for me, and then give me the gist? Thanks.

So last summer I poured boiling water over all the ants in my garden, and all the uncles were furious.

Pundamentalist

Dad always said it was up to fat people to help themselves, which is why he ran a carvery.

A dyslexic friend of mine tried to book himself a room at an Ibis and ended up blowing himself up for Alan.

Recently I've been pulling out all the stops, and as a result there's been a lot more accidents at junctions.

I can't wait for the garden centre to open.
I've been living on borrowed thyme.

There's a lot of conspiracy theories around nowadays, or is that just what they want us to believe?

Gary Delaney

I can't believe I've invented a cure for self-harming. Sometimes I have to pinch myself.

I'd tell you who the most ungrateful person I know is, but I don't think he'd thank me for it.

Yes I could go to a fancy dress party dressed as the leaning tower of Pisa, if I was so inclined.

I used to work at the Velcro factory making hooks. We never got on the with the people making loops though, as there was a lot of friction between us.

At first I didn't realise how many children were in my class, as it took a while to register.

Pundamentalist

Ridiculous! I had a bit of a falling out with one of the other members, and apparently now I'm no longer welcome at Hot Air Ballooning Club.

I was telling my therapist how I always seem to misjudge situations, and he replied, 'Are you going to buy that couch or not?'

My wife asked me to pick her up a blusher in Boots, so I came back with an easily embarrassed farmer.

I don't think I've ever cleaned my bathroom mirror, which is something that reflects very badly on me.

I don't know how long my model railway is now, I've lost track.

I can't seem to find one of my famous rapper action figures. No Biggie.

Narcissists need to take a long, hard look at themselves.

I was going to do a gag about social distancing, but it's a bit of an inside joke.

There's nothing I love more than a cup of builder's tea in the morning. The hard part is not spilling it as you run away from the builder.

Cleopatra's Needle. Good point, well made.

Pundamentalist

Do I use words that sound like sneezes?
No, I eschew them.

A friend of mine has recently come out as
pansexual, which is alarming, as I lent him one
of my pans.

Find out your porn star name by coming to the
disused warehouse in Romford, 3pm this Tuesday,
and asking for Gary.

A friend of mine's got shifty eyes, which means
he reads everything in block capitals.

Shazam but for who your mum's talking about and
how you're supposed to know them.

Gary Delaney

I'm not very good at dwarf impressions.
Still, heh ho.

Winnie the Pooh, possibly the most vindictive
chapter in Nelson Mandela's autobiography.

People had a go at Keith Chegwin, but Swap Shop
was a game changer.

Ann Summers was so busy after lockdown they
had to operate on a first served, first come basis.

I'm not saying I'm boring, but I took a personality
test and it came back negative.

Pundamentalist

Bit embarrassing. The S fell off my Speedos so now it says Speedo.

Marks and Spencer was founded 100 years ago today. Many happy returns!

. . . and now the results for the Musketeers' football league:

4-1

4-1

4-1

4-1

4-1

and 4-4.

Gary Delaney

I can't believe the government are relying on models to forecast the pandemic. They should ask scientists instead. They're not as pretty but they know a lot more.

I looked up déjà vu in the dictionary and there was a picture of me looking up déjà vu in the dictionary.

I like to work alone as a trapeze artist. I used to have a partner, but I had to let him go.

I got a nasty shock from a bathroom light switch once. I turned it on and saw my dad having a dump.

Pundamentalist

I thought I saw Idris Elba in town earlier, but it turned out it was just Idris Arse.

I left some Scotch eggs in the fridge for too long, and now they've hatched into tiny Scottish people.

I just made myself a bacon sandwich. I must be the worst wizard ever.

Apostrophe's.

Ampers&.

Romeo and Juliet. Then Romeo paid the bill.

It turns out 'working from home' is only wrong by two letters.

Shit a brick! I think they've found out how I've been stealing from the Lego factory.

My mum carried on working as a librarian when she was pregnant with me. Unfortunately I was three weeks overdue, which cost her 20p.

I think it's a missed opportunity that at no point in any Scandinavian crime drama has anyone ever said, 'It's a fair cop'.

I fisted a ventriloquist once to see how he liked it.

Pundamentalist

Last night I watched a really interesting
documentary about pirates on the iiPlayer.

I used to work in customer services at Ann
Summers, but the people there gave me bad vibes.

I nearly got fired on my first day making Barbie
and Ken dolls for giving them genitals, but luckily
I managed to smooth things over.

If I was reincarnated as a fish and caught by a
trawler I'd be gutted.

If you watch a porn film backwards it's about a
man who hoovers spunk off a woman, then breaks
her washing machine and leaves.

Gary Delaney

I've spent all my money on the world's biggest
pack of cards, and now it's up to me to deal with it.

Apparently 'Dance like no one is watching' doesn't
mean 'With your cock out'.

I've just been told they can't remove the shrapnel
in my leg. It's a bit of a bombshell.

I really must stop stealing nuns' dirty clothes.
It's a filthy habit.

The bad news is I can't find my proper Ouija board,
but the good news is the spirits say I'm going to
buy a house in Mayfair for £200.

Pundamentalist

Quick straw poll: Who likes straw?

People criticise me for covering myself in jam,
but it's an act of self-preservation.

I failed again in my attempt to become Chair of
the Hula Hoop Society. I guess I just don't move in
the right circles.

I tell you who'd make a fitting statue, The Artist
Formerly Known as Plinth.

I tell you who really bug me, spies.

The reason there's never been a Rolling Stones
musical is that it's so hard to finding a casting
director without sin.

Does anyone want to invest their life savings in my perfume factory? You know it makes scents.

One time I drank champagne from a stripper's shoe and promptly passed out. I found out later it had been laced.

I complained to the wine club that their last delivery hadn't even been pressed and fermented properly, but they said it was just a case of sour grapes.

I was never a fan of organ donation, but then I had a change of heart.

I'm auditioning for a role in a play about a man out walking his dog. Hopefully they'll give me the lead.

Pundamentalist

I bet the Queen was disappointed to watch 'One Flew Over the Cuckoo's Nest', and find it wasn't about the time she flew over a cuckoo's nest.

My Roger Moore look-alike competition has certainly raised a few eyebrows.

'Can I borrow some of your chloroform?'
'Sure, knock yourself out.'

Not only am I bringing sexy back, but it's still in its original packaging and I've got the receipt.

I've met more Morris Dancers than I could shake a stick at.

I'm always careful to fully insert my card into the reader, which makes me popular at tills, but less so in libraries.

I saw two men fighting over a crossword clue (2 down, 'altercation', 8 letters). I told them violence is not the answer.

I don't want to tempt fete, but there's a patch of ground near me that would be perfect for some sort of outdoor event.

Not a lot people know this about 50 Cent, but he used to be one half of Dollar.

I'm prone to a bit of comfort eating, and also the odd Persil tablet.

Pundamentalist

I tried reading a book on premature ejaculation,
but I couldn't get past the opening passage.

I think MC Hammer and Jimmy Nail should form a
double act, and call themselves MC Jimmy.

If I leave my light on and the window open, how
many insects will fly in? You do the moths.

If anybody steals my identity, at least I'll know
who to look for.

To those who have accused me of being an
apologist, I can only say sorry.

Gary Delaney

I've just filled in and posted the form to become an organ donor. Signed, sealed, de-livered.

The label on this loaf of bread says that two slices contain as much calcium as a glass of milk, so now I just need to find out which two.

Amazingly, it's still completely legal to kidnap a mother superior. No offence, nun taken.

My flatmate's a naturist. It's not something I'm into, but at least I can see his point.

Sometimes I like to go birdwatching, just for larks.

Pundamentalist

Maybe Jesus' face just looked a lot like toast?

I read that a 102-year-old woman has just earned a history degree. Surely that's cheating?

I told an estate agent to go to hell. He said, 'Actually, we call it "lower heaven".'

I thought a friend of mine looked like a vampire, but on reflection he doesn't.

Can anyone fix my deep sea diver's suit?
No pressure.

Gary Delaney

I feel like I really broke down some barriers at work today, so I'm not the most popular person at the Safari Park.

I accidentally used a volume maximising shampoo, and now my hair's too noisy.

I feel guilty because I shoplifted Trivial Pursuit even though I've no one to play it with. I'm going to have to ask myself some very difficult questions.

Grandad was afraid of change, but if anything that just made us throw it harder.

My friend insists I should refer to her new job as a 'Primary School Health Outreach Worker', but I think it's just nit-picking really.

Pundamentalist

My nose was all clogged up this morning, so
I gave it a really good blow, and two wooden shoes
popped out.

I stole a neck brace from the hospital. I feel kinda
bad, but at least I can hold my head up high.

There's a deleted scene in the original Terminator
film where a T-800 tries to gain access to a
resistance base, but is foiled when they can't say
which of these 9 pictures contains a motorbike.

If Tim Berners-Lee had the internet, he'd never
have invented the internet.

Ruin an orgy by shouting 'winner stays on'.

Gary Delaney

My spiritualist says that in a past life I was really gullible.

Of all the Greek gods Hermes is my favourite. I love all the stories of how he doesn't turn up, can't find the right house and carelessly throws packages into a puddle.

Married men, a great way to remember your password is to choose something you've done wrong, because that way your wife will never let you forget it.

If you're fed up with strange men groping you on busy trains, then rest assured I know how you feel.

Pundamentalist

Why do you never see female mimes? I think it's because there's a glass ceiling.

It was hard work being a Customs Officer. I had to start at the bottom, and then work my way up.

'I'd like a return ticket to Belgium please.'
'Antwerp?'
'No, my husband's not coming.'

I used to do a joke about being a terrible midwife, but I struggled with the delivery.

The wife and I have started thinking seriously about adoption, so we spoke to the agency, but unfortunately nobody wanted to take our kids.

Gary Delaney

Sad news. Today we lost the inventor of the protractor. He's with the angles now.

Whenever people ask about my wife I always say, 'She's with Jesus now', which is technically true as she left me for a Spanish bloke.

Just sat my A levels again naked. Living the dream!

Well, stone the crows! I'm in trouble with the RSPB again.

This year I'm going to do dry January, and see if I can manage an entire month without any foreplay.

Pundamentalist

I told my girlfriend I love Pixar films and I haven't
actually got any, so I think it's time to own Up.

It's called 'Getting your guns out' because you have
the right to bare arms.

I tried to buy a second hand jetski off a Russian,
and now I own a plane.

My wife says I have a tendency to overdramatise
things, so she clearly hates me.

My wife said she wanted to put the magic back
in our sex life, and then pulled a rabbit out of her
wizard's sleeve.

I'm beached body ready.

Duck billed platypus, platypus paid duck.

I was buying a new jacket. The shop assistant said, 'Would you like to try it on?' I said, 'Sure, what time do you finish work?'

Opening up Google and forgetting what you wanted to look up is the new walking into a room and forgetting what you went in for.

Stupid birds outside are singing so loudly I can't hear my 'Relaxing Birdsong' CD.

Pundamentalist

I spent this morning swanning around the town
centre. I hissed at people and broke a man's arm.

People who say power is an aphrodisiac have
clearly never tried putting their cock in a socket.

I entered a competition to be fluffer of the year,
but unfortunately I only made the semis.

This cook book says you can make anything thicker
by adding cornflour, so I've been rubbing it into my
penis for three weeks now.

I once had a fling with a woman in John Lewis.
She said I was amazing in soft furnishings, but
a bit disappointing in the trouser department.

The best way to console a pedant is by saying they're, their, there.

The main difficulty with carbon dating is you can end up with coal all over your knob.

Pigeon fanciers are so called because it sounds a lot better than chicken fucker.

Despite the name, AA Milne was not actually a Scouser.

POW camps got their name from the fact that captured soldiers were forced to spend their days adding captions to Batman comics.

Pundamentalist

The Metamorphosis isn't the only book in which a man wakes up one morning to discover he's suddenly become a beetle for no good reason. There's also Ringo Starr's autobiography.

To be honest I found my rescue dog disappointing. He couldn't even climb a ladder, never mind drive a fire engine.

Probably the most famous wardrobe malfunction ever was that one where those kids ended up in Narnia.

If you rub a dock leaf on Sting he will disappear.

The Rock was the most successful wrestler in the history of WWE before finally being beaten by a mysterious character known only as 'The Paper'.

Twerking is what a Yorkshireman does to earn T'wages.

The best thing about healthy meals is I've loads of space to eat all the sausages in the fridge an hour later because I'm so fucking hungry.

Once a year I like to stay up late to watch the Oscars, usually until about 5am, when Mr Oscar closes their bedroom curtains.

Pundamentalist

When it comes to speeding I really have to put my foot down.

The more I read about confirmation bias, the more I think it might be true.

There comes a time when a man should stop and reflect on all the little mistakes he's made in his life. Or as it's more commonly known, Father's Day.

I kept hearing this annoying knocking noise coming from underneath my car. So I got out to have a look, turned out I'd run over Jehovah's Witness.

Gary Delaney

I used to try to make eye contact with people
on the tube, but one thing I soon learned about
Londoners is they hate you touching their eyes.

On Valentine's my girlfriend she got all upset
when she found out that I'd wiped my knob on the
box of chocolates I'd given her. Luckily I managed
to come out of it smelling of roses.

The hardest part of growing up narcoleptic was
working out how many sleeps 'til Christmas.

The Queen's Speech should really be called
'The One Show'.

Pundamentalist

Last year instead of wasting money on presents
I sent a goat to a village in Africa. He had a lovely
time and wants to go again this year.

I went to buy a Christmas tree and the guy said,
'Are you going to put it up yourself?' I said, 'No
I was thinking the living room.'

Just seen Chris Rea on my train. Liar!

Lots of surprises from the family this Christmas.
Apparently Dad's gay, Nan's dead and I'm adopted.

The OCD Society Christmas Carol singalong was
going really well, right up until, 'He's making a list,
he's checking it twice . . .'

Gary Delaney

I've already got all my Christmas presents bought and wrapped! On a completely unrelated note, how long can puppies survive without water?

Every Christmas day we always have pigs in blankets, or as you probably call it, relatives sleeping in the spare room.

It's tradition in our family that we always have a Christmas jumper, and then it's my job to talk them down.

I didn't know what to get my little niece for Christmas so I asked my sister what she's into, apparently at the moment she's mad about frozen stuff so I got her some oven chips and peas.

Pundamentalist

On Christmas morning we'd always wake up
and go, 'Has he been? Has he been?' Because we
knew dad wouldn't put the presents out until after
he'd had a shit.

This Christmas I'm taking the whole family to
Lapland, which is great, because normally those
clubs don't let kids in.

I always think 'A Muppets Christmas Carol' sounds
like Danny Dyer describing an inferior version of
the Dickens classic.

Q: What's white and falls from the sky at
Christmas?
A: Emo kids.

Q: What would Beyoncé be called if she married Roy Castle?

A: Necrophiliac.

I've got an irregular heartbeat, pa rum pa pum pum.

The greatest trick Santa ever played was convincing the world he doesn't exist.

'What was that Chris Rea song? The one all about a man driving home for Xmas?'

'The Road to Hell?'

'Yes, that's it'.

Pundamentalist

Frankincense was actually the name of the perfume's creator.

I bought a Travelodge advent calendar. It's still got chocolate in, but you can't open the windows.

I bought a Microsoft advent calendar, you open too many windows at once, and they all shut again for no fucking reason.

Will Ferrell has announced that he is to star in a sequel to 'Elf' called 'Zwölf'.

In my last job I just used to punch buttons all day, which is why I'm no longer allowed to do panto.

Gary Delaney

Whenever I see a respected actor in Panto, I always like to shout, 'It's beneath you'.

It's a struggle putting up visiting relatives over Christmas, but so much cheaper than traditional decorations.

Panto news: Aladdin has been fired after testing positive for performance enhancing rugs.

This year I'm doing Vagueanuary. I'm giving something up, I'm just not sure what it is.

I gave up drinking on the 1st of January. It's better for your health, and it's only one day a year.

Pundamentalist

I'm not saying Jools Holland's Hootenanny is recorded well in advance, but the surprise guests this year are Prince and David Bowie.

Sure everyone cares about straws killing dolphins now, but they've been breaking camels' backs for years.

Genius is 1% inspiration and 99% perspiration, which explains why Prince Andrew is so stupid.

Sad news: the British simile champion has died. We shall not see his like again.

My mum doesn't trust my Dad's secretary. I asked her why, and she just said, 'I've seen her type before.'

Gary Delaney

Today someone told me that I look good
with a salt and pepper beard, so I took that
as a condiment.

One time I told my little brother that hydrochloric
acid tastes just like lemonade and he hasn't
spoken to me since.

I've just written a book.
It didn't take long, it was only two words.

Acknowledgements

Many thanks to:

Sarah, for putting up with me tuning her out whenever I get an idea for a joke and for generally being my rock, my inspiration and for teaching me to be positive. And also for not minding that I used the dedication space in the front of the book to squeeze in an extra joke instead of dedicating it to her, which I clearly should have done really. I've just read this out loud to her and she whispered to the dog 'I did mind'.

Lieutenant Ripley, Chief Brody and Commander Tuvok for sitting with me while I wrote many of these jokes.

Christian, Ben and everyone else at Blue Book AM, and to Rowan at The Soho Agency for helping make this book happen.

Richard at Headline for seeing the Tweet: 'Hey everyone, did I mention that I've got a book coming out? I don't know why I shoved it up there in the first place' – and then making it happen, editing into something readable, and putting up with me being late and awkward.

Gary Delaney

The idiot who ate a bat and gave me the time off to write this book. Without their help I never could have waded through 20 years' worth of notebooks, old phones, scraps of paper, tens of thousands of old tweets and gig recordings to make this collection.

All the unwitting editors who've ever sat in my audiences or followed me on social media.

Everyone who has ever been to see me on tour, or is coming to my big post-covid tour, especially if they found out about the dates by signing up to my mailing list at www.garydelaney.com. Don't worry, I don't think anyone has noticed that this bit is just an advert for my forthcoming tour, which will be great and all new jokes.

Particular thanks to those who've directly or indirectly taught me how to write jokes: Emo Philips, Harry Hill, Lee and Herring, Mitch Hedberg, Steven Wright, Anthony Jeselnik, Henny Youngman, Max Miller, Ken Dodd, Simon Munnery, Rohan Agalawatta, Jimmy Carr, Milton Jones, Tim Vine, Shelagh Martin, Gene Peret, Melvin Helitzer, Caimh McDonnell, Dominic English, Chris Longridge and Sarah again.